Pain With A Purpose

Pain With A Purpose

DR. CHERYL R. SMITH

Copyright © 2012 by Dr. Cheryl R. Smith.

Library of Congress Control Number: 2012903993
ISBN: Hardcover   978-1-4691-7855-4
                Softcover   978-1-4691-7854-7
                Ebook   978-1-4691-7856-1

All rights reserved. No part of this book may be reproduced or transmitted in any form or by any means, electronic or mechanical, including photocopying, recording, or by any information storage and retrieval system, without permission in writing from the copyright owner.

This book was printed in the United States of America.

To order additional copies of this book, contact:
Xlibris Corporation
1-888-795-4274
www.Xlibris.com
Orders@Xlibris.com
113230

CONTENTS

ACKNOWLEDGEMENTS 9

PREFACE   A Gethsemane Moment 11

CHAPTER 1   Acknowledging Your Pain 13

CHAPTER 2   Understanding The Purpose Of Your Pain 21

CHAPTER 3   Accepting The Process Of Your Pain 25

CHAPTER 4   From Hurting To Healing 29

CHAPTER 5   This Pain May Be Real, But It Is Not Unto Death 32

CHAPTER 6   This Is Just Temporary 35

CHAPTER 7   Surely, There Is An End To This! 38

CHAPTER 8   Rename Your Place Of Pain 41

CHAPTER 9   In The Meantime, Celebrate 43

CHAPTER 10   This Pain Is Birthing Something New 46

DEDICATION

This book is dedicated to all the children who have experienced abuse; mothers who have lost children either through miscarriage or other forms of death; women or men who have been hurt in a love relationship. This is written for husbands or wives who have had to grieve over the death of a spouse; children who have been neglected or abandoned by a parent; family members who have had to grieve the loss of a loved one or anyone who experienced molestation, rape or hurt of any kind and had to learn to move forward.

ACKNOWLEDGEMENTS

WRITING A BOOK is not always an easy task because during the course of your life if you are as busy as I am, you have many diversions. However, this has been an extremely rewarding process and although it took me a little while to get through this, I am glad I did it. I started this after trying to work through the process of the death of my brother, but I had to put it down and come back to it when I was ready in my effort to help someone else through his or her painful process.

I have to honor God for being God and for allowing me the opportunity to do this. The prophetic word concerning this has been coming to me for years so I am grateful for the manifestation.

Special thanks to my husband, James who has always been a tremendous support and has loved me through some rough places! Thank you for sticking it out with me. I believe in a lot of ways we have brought healing to each other.

To my daughter Lisa, who noticed my pain over the loss of my brother and was 13 yrs. old at the time, but was not afraid to reach out and say, "There is a purpose to this." Thank you. That helped me arrive to this point.

My parents, Bishop Richard Pender, Sr. and Patricia Pender, thanks for always encouraging, loving and supporting me in all of my endeavors and projects.

Thanks to all of my friends and well wishers who have supported me down through the years, especially my sister-friend, Leslie. Thanks for all the "Checking on you" texts, calls, and emails. Even with miles between us, you have never ceased to support and encourage me. It has impacted my life. Love you!

I would like to acknowledge my Church family, Emmanuel Worship and Deliverance Center for all of your encouragement and prayers.

Thanks to my Godmother, Wahseeola Evans, who has always supported me in my efforts to achieve.

I have many Godchildren whom I love dearly but special thanks goes out to Ayeisha and Andre for the role they played in making sure that I stuck with this project and followed it all the way through. You were apart of making this happen so thank you.

I would also like to acknowledge the memory of some people who have gone on before me, but were vital to who I have become and supported me 100% in whatever I did—Apostle Robert Evans, Jr., my grandmothers Sylvia Evans and Corrine Pender, and my # 1 fan, my brother Richard Pender, Jr. I will always love you all and I am proud to have had you in my life! The impact you have had on my life continues!

I would also like to say to anyone I have ever hurt that I am sorry and to anyone that has ever hurt me, I forgive you. You will see that is all a part of the healing and wholeness process.

PREFACE

A Gethsemane Moment

I HAVE ALWAYS been an observant person and it is interesting how I am looking all around me and it is clear that there are many of us who find ourselves in some crazy places right now. These places do not make sense—places that have caused us to experience a sense of frustration, discomfort, or suffering like never before. Sometimes these places seem so overwhelming that we find ourselves where Jesus was in Matthew 26. He was in the Garden of Gethsemane and was so deeply distressed and distraught that he said in verse 38, *"My soul is exceedingly sorrowful."* This place was difficult and overwhelming, yet necessary for the sake of purpose. This place was part of his process. Gethsemane represents the place of pressing and crushing. Gethsemane is the place where you find yourself surrounded by people, but still alone. Gethsemane is the place where you become overwhelmed by the process and the assignment. Yet Gethsemane is the place that you have to endure in order to embrace the next level.

What signifies your Gethsemane? You get a doctor's report that is not good, mishandled on the job, trouble in the home, overwhelmed by bills, worried about what is going on with your children, financial problems, frustrated by relationships, family in an uproar, confusion all around, grief, people just do not seem to want to act right and the list goes on. You are not alone; I have been there lately too—at that place of crushing and pressing.

The diagnosis is you are just having a Gethsemane Moment. It is the kind of moment where you find yourself in a *"Father if it be thou will let this cup pass from me . . ."* You see this cup represents a place of struggle, a place of frustration, a place of discomfort, a place of separation. Even Jesus experienced some anxiety about the intensity of this place, but God could not do anything different because to lessen the process would lessen the greatness of his purpose. It is the same with us. Where you are is a part of your process and even though it is making no sense and at times quite painful, it is working together for your good. That which seems crazy and overwhelming has purpose and it is pushing you towards destiny.

You must also note that in a Gethsemane Moment you will find yourself in a struggle between life and death, if not physically then mentally and emotionally. You will find yourself trying to fight and stand up under the pressure, but unable to do it in your own strength. The thing is you try to bring other people, your inner circle, into your process, but they fall asleep under the pressure, in other words they are unconscious to where you are and what you are really facing. The reality is it is not their process; it is yours. Some places you have to walk by yourself. The only way to survive this place is to embrace the strength of the Lord; in other words, your way through it is in prayer. You get through it by praying like Jesus prayed. ". . . Not my will but thy will be done." You can not pray an ordinary prayer in this place, but one that will shift your place of suffering to a place of strength and your place of anxiety to a place of peace. Luke 22 says in the Garden of Gethsemane Jesus prayed so intensely that the sweat became like drops of blood falling to the ground. Even in that, God was faithful because even though he did not deliver him out of it, He strengthened him to get through it for the sake of purpose. It is called **Pain with a Purpose**. Do not fret about where you are; you are just having a Gethsemane Moment. There is purpose in this and if you pray, God will reveal some things to you while strengthening you to walk through it.

CHAPTER 1

Acknowledging Your Pain

HAVE YOU EVER had a paper cut? In general the wound is small, but don't be deceived by its size because it can produce significant pain. Then you have the larger wounds or gashes that not only produce pain, but are also accompanied by blood. No matter what size the wound, the pain is real and how we handle the hurt determines how we heal.

Merriam-Webster defines pain as "localized physical suffering associated with bodily disorder (as a disease or an injury)." It is "acute mental or emotional distress or suffering." (*www.merriam-webster.com*) This definition is exemplary of many of the situations in our lives that have caused us pain. No matter what has caused the pain or how intense the pain, you must acknowledge it if you want to be healed.

In I Kings 3, we see the story of two prostitutes. In the text they have both recently experienced the joy of childbirth. I am sure this was a wonderful experience because now they finally had someone to love that would love them back. These women had been willing victims of men who abused their bodies. They were probably hurting emotionally because they would sleep with one man after another night after night. They were looking for love in the wrong places and now they had found love in the birthing of a child. Undoubtedly birthing a child probably was a boost to their self-esteem because it gave them something to be proud about.

The women came before the King because one of them had rolled over in her sleep and accidentally smothered her child and now the baby was dead. The woman awoke in the middle of the night and took the other woman's living son replacing him with her dead son. When the other woman awoke the next day, she awoke to a dead child, but she knew that it was not her child, so she took the matter before the King.

Let's pause here for a moment. The woman whose son had died had to be hurting really deeply. This was the son that she had carried and waited for 9 months and now he was dead. Yet, she showed no remorse at the death of her child nor did she show any with taking someone else's child and claiming that it was hers. She was in pain, but she was in denial.

Her pain and denial was so intense that when the king said that he would use the sword to kill the living child and give each mother a portion of the child, she still showed no remorse. She was willing to let the living child die, but his real mother was willing to give him up so that he could live. The first woman's refusal to acknowledge her loss made her numb to her own pain. Many of us are in pain, yet we walk around in denial. You cannot deal with pain that you suppress or won't acknowledge. The reality is if you do not acknowledge it, the situation could become worse.

Let's look at another Biblical example. In Genesis 4, we are introduced to Cain and Abel, two brothers. Abel was a shepherd and Cain was a farmer, a tiller of the ground. Cain became envious of Abel when they both made a sacrifice—an offering unto God. Abel's sacrifice was accepted but Cain's was not. The Bible says that Cain became angry and *"his countenance fell"*. In other words, he felt rejected. This was the root of his pain—rejection. He was feeling passed over, discarded, overlooked, which takes me to a point that is worth discussing. **Pain that is not properly treated may not heal properly.**

A few of years ago I was on a vacation and I fell and injured my ankle. My ankle was swollen and I could not walk on it. This was day 3 of a 7-day vacation, so I had to get some medical help before my husband and I returned home. I went to a doctor there and after examining my foot; he diagnosed it as a bad ankle sprain. He wrapped my ankle in an ace bandage, prescribed some pain medicine, gave me an ice pack and some crutches, and told me to keep it elevated for a couple of days. By the end of the vacation, I was still unable to put any pressure on my foot and my husband suggested that we see another doctor when we returned home.

Two days after we returned home, I went to another doctor. After they took x-rays and a MRI, it was diagnosed that it was a fracture, not a sprain. After the fracture healed, it was later determined that 2 ligaments in my ankle were also severed and needed to be repaired. As a result of it not being treated properly at the time that the injury occurred, I had to have a surgery that I may not have had to have on my foot. The improper treatment prolonged my pain, delayed my healing, and cost me more money for extensive treatment. Again I repeat, a pain not properly treated may not heal properly and as a result may cause you more pain in the long run.

In addition to that, **untreated pain can alter your behavior and cause you to respond in a negative or irrational manner.** Cain's pain had a chain reaction. The rejection led to anger, which festered, into bitterness, which turned into hatred, which eventually drove Cain to murder his brother, Abel. His pain was never treated and as a result it got worse leading to destructive behavior.

Another point of interest is that **unresolved pain can lead to permanent or irreversible consequences.** Once Cain killed Abel, he could not change what happened. He had to live with the knowledge and the guilt of killing his own brother. His action had a permanent result, which led to permanent consequences. He was cursed from the earth, as a fugitive and his occupation became much harder.

By Genesis 6, God was so upset and disappointed with man. In verses 6 and 7 it says, *"And it repented the lord that he had made man on the earth, and it grieved him at his heart. And the Lord said, I will destroy man whom I have created from the face of the earth;"* Sin entered the land and became a contagious disease that was infecting everyone—everyone accept Noah and his family. As with any other contagious disease, it had to be contained and God felt the only way to do this was to destroy carriers, who had now become the source. In the midst of all of this, he found favor with Noah and had him build an ark to protect him and his family from the flood he was sending to destroy the earth. So it was that after Noah built the ark, he, his family, and 2 of every living thing entered the ark. Genesis 7 allows us to know that all-living things that were on the dry land died as a result of the flood.

Now you might ask, what does this story have to do with the statement that unresolved pain can lead to permanent results and consequences? Well the reality is that sin is a disease that can cause pain. A person that sins generally is a person in pain whether they acknowledge it or not. The root of their sin often times comes from the fact that they are not being fulfilled in some area of their lives. They respond as if something is missing and they need more. Sin is really an appetite out of control. It is like you are saying you need more or you need something else outside of what has already been provided for you. Because of sin man was destroyed. That was the result. That was the consequence and it was permanent because those destroyed were not brought back. The results of the flood were catastrophic.

Something else important to note is that **pain that is hidden cannot be healed.** If you masquerade pain it sometimes gets worse. This is why we have people walking around as dysfunctional adults. Some event in their childhood caused them pain and because of the intensity of the pain, they decided to hide it and act like it did not happen. The result of that decision has left them having to deal with a trauma or traumatic event that has affected them their entire life. This issue of hiding pain dates back to biblical times. In II Samuel 13, David's son, Amnon, plots to rape his sister, Tamar. Then after he rapes her, he despises and rejects her by sending her away harshly and abruptly from his home. Then when her other brother, Absalom, finds out he tells her not to tell anyone. He tells her to keep quiet even though she has been the victim of a crime. He tells her to hold her peace and not tell anyone about what happened because he believed that what goes on in the family, stays in the family. He did not want the family name to be ridiculed. He did not want any shame to be brought to the family name, but what about her shame?

Let's break this down. What exactly do we have here? We have a young woman who was raped by her brother, a victim of incest. Her pain was not just a result of being violated, but it was also caused by the guilt and shame that she experienced as a result of the violation. Then on top of that, she could not tell anyone. She must have felt broken inside, not only from what happened to her, but also from how her family reacted. The brother that did this to her now resents her and sends her away, her other brother tells her to hide it, and her father is angry, but does nothing to avenge her. She was daddy's little girl—you would think he would have responded differently to someone harming his daughter, but David did nothing to punish his son. According to the law, Amnon should have been put to death for this immoral act, but nothing was done (at least not by David).

This probably is not unlike things that happen today. A child is raped by someone that he or she knows. When they get the courage to tell someone they trust, it is covered up, but cover-ups are open wounds that are not healed. You have got to deal with the issues in your life that are causing you pain. Hiding them, covering them will not make it go away—it only makes it worse.

Tamar was devastated by all of this. Her virginity had been stolen and there appeared to be no redemption in sight. II Samuel 13:20 says, *"... so Tamar remained desolate in her brother Absalom's house."* The word desolate refers to being in ruin. Her life was destroyed, so much so that she physically went in hiding in her brother's house. She remained a victim of her pain because she chose to hide it.

This was Tamar's story—her pain, but let's look at yours. To the child being abused or dealing with having been abused, if you keep it to yourself and don't deal with it, you cannot heal. To the wife/husband involved in spousal abuse, if you do not speak out about it and get some help, you will not heal. To the family member stricken with grief over the loss of a loved one, if you try to ignore the pain of the loss, you will not heal. I know. I've been there with the loss of my own brother. I walked around for months nearly numb from trying to hide the pain of the loss. I figured that it was more important that I help everyone else deal with their pain and I did it for so long that it was like I was becoming a walking zombie. The problem with that was the longer I did that, the worse the pain became. One day, I became so overwhelmed that I felt like I was losing control of reality and I started shaking and could not stop. As I began to pray, I broke and everything that I had been holding inside just came out like a flood. From that day I was able to deal with the pain a little more each day, until it became manageable. However, I am clear that if God had not intervened, I probably would have lost my mind because the pain of that lost had become too much for me and hiding it was harming me. The interesting part was that other people were around me literally watching me self-destruct, but unaware because of the facade. I will say it again because it bears repeating, if you try to hide pain it can get worse. Pain that is hidden is harder to heal. If you want to be healed, you have got to deal with your pain and sometimes that requires seeking help. It also requires you identifying the cause of your pain, so that it can be properly treated.

You have got to realize that pain is often a symptom of a greater problem or condition so if you ignore it, the problem could get worse. For example, when I was 19 years old, I had this pain on the right side of my abdomen. The pain was a sign, a symptom that something was wrong; something was going on in my body that was not normal. As I continued to try to ignore the pain and move ahead with my daily functions, the pain grew worse—more intense, so much so that I could barely walk. By then there were other symptoms that were accompanying the pain—high fever, loss of appetite, fatigue, and vomiting. Finally, I went to the doctor and he sent me directly to the hospital to have emergency surgery. My appendix was perforated and was beginning to release poison into my body. I had been having the pain off and on for about a month, but the last 2 weeks it became more intense and was followed by the other symptoms. If I had gone to the doctor before, then maybe they could have performed the surgery before it began releasing the poison and I would not have been in the hospital for almost a month. Ignoring the pain made the condition worse. The reality is had I ignored it any longer I may not have been around now to write about it. You must deal with pain. You cannot ignore it. You cannot hide it. You must deal with pain if you want to be healed.

Another thing that you should know about pain is that **sometimes you can be in pain for so long that it seems normal.** It is like you no longer realize that you are in pain, but you are. David's entire family was in pain, but I am not even sure that they realized it because it had been going on for so long. David's pain began as a child with rejection from his father. As he grew older, he had to deal with the pain of betrayal from his mentor, Saul. Then he had to deal with the pain of losing his son as an infant because of his immoral actions with Bathsheba. Now in II Samuel 13 through 18 he has to deal with the pain and agony of watching 3 of his other children self-destruct and once again he is at the root of it. His actions with Bathsheba and Uriah brought a curse on his family. II Samuel 13 through 18 is the fulfillment of this curse. Absalom was so angry with his brother, Amnon for what he did to Tamar that he murdered him. Absalom's pain was a symptom of his bitterness and resentment. This resentment, first with Amnon now turned toward his father and became so intense that he planned a conspiracy against David. Absalom's resentment and bitterness turned on him and as a result he died a tragic death. So, once again David had to deal with the loss of a child, actually two children, and face the fact that indirectly, he had something to do with it.

David had been in pain for so long, that I don't even think he realized it. Pain began to be a part of his daily life. You don't want to deal with pain for so long that it becomes a normal phenomenon or you become numb to it. When pain gets to that point, you could be ignoring something that is a symptom of a greater problem. If it gets to this point, you might want to analyze why you have become numb. For example, let's say you have a pain in your foot or leg. As a result of that pain, you develop a limp. You continue trying to walk, but every step you take is with a limp. After a while, if it is not treated, that limp becomes your normal everyday walk, so much so until you no longer realize that you are limping.

The interesting thing about pain with a limp is that although it may slow you down, it does not stop you from moving. David's pain had a limp, but it did not stop him. This is why he was not always able to recognize that he was in pain, because with every traumatic experience, he kept moving. His ability to keep moving inspite of the pain was deceiving him. Somebody else can relate to this kind of pain because you have experienced it. The wife that discovers that her husband is having an affair or the husband that discovers that his wife is having an affair; he or she understands this concept of pain with a limp, especially if they have children. They are in pain and sometimes the pain slows them down, but they try to keep moving because it's the only way they know how to survive and keep it together.

Another example of this concept is the young person with the eating disorder. It is pain with a limp, whether it is anorexia, bulimia, or purging. No matter what event in your life has caused this pain, if it does not kill you, you have learned to live with it and keep moving. Even if the eating disorder slows you down, you try to keep moving because again, it's the only way you know how to survive. So, what do you do? You keep moving even with a limp. You have been in pain for so long that it seems normal, but it is not.

On a side note, you have got to be careful that you don't allow your pain or condition to name you. If you are not careful, that condition will hang around so long that it will begin to define who you are. People will start to identify you by your condition. Take a look in the scriptures. There were a lot of people who struggled with conditions for so long that they became identified by them. Some examples of this are the man with an infirmity at the pool of Bethesda, the woman with the issue of blood, blind Bartimaeus, the man with a dumb spirit, a man full of leprosy, the lame man at the gate, the woman possessed with a spirit of divination, and it does not stop here. All of these people struggled with a condition for so long that the condition became the thing that identified them. It became so much a part of them that we never even knew most of their real names. It became a label for them that when people saw them, they acknowledged them by their condition.

To break this concept down in our terms, instead of being known as Sally, you become Sally, the liar or Johnny, the fornicator, or Rob, the man who had two children with one woman while being married to someone else, or Joan, the teenager who had a baby, or Joe, the drug addict, or the man or woman struggling with unnatural affections, or Dan, the church gigolo, or Jan, the girl with a reputation of being easy, etc. Although the names are fictitious in that I don't know anyone with these names that has these conditions attached to them, the conditions themselves are real. Someone has been struggling with a condition for so long that you are beginning to be identified by it.

It is time to seek a higher authority. It is time to put your condition on the altar. Don't allow the pain to change your name! The interesting part about the biblical characters named by their conditions is that when the condition was gone, so were they. You don't hear any more about them, because they had become their condition. It was like the condition was what made them significant or noteworthy. Don't allow your condition to alter your identity! Your purpose is greater than your condition! It's time to be healed. It's time to be set free. It's time to be made whole and only God can do this.

The bottom line is you have to deal with your pain. You cannot hide it. You cannot ignore it and you don't want to become it. You must acknowledge the pain and deal with it if you want to be healed.

CHAPTER 2

Understanding The Purpose Of Your Pain

WE HAVE DISCUSSED different types of pain and the importance of not becoming a victim of your pain, but it is also important to deal with the cause of your pain. One way to better understand this is to understand and know the purpose of your pain.

Purpose has to do with a specific intention or result. Ecclesiastes 3:1 says, *"To everything there is a season, and a time to every purpose under the heaven . . ."* Everything has a purpose and a season and your pain is not exempt from this. Your pain is not intended to last forever, but it does have a specific purpose. Think about it, if you had not had that headache with the blurry vision, you might not have had your eyesight examined. Take me for example, if I did not have that pain in my lower abdomen I might not have had the surgery and would not have known that my body was in danger. That pain had a purpose of signaling that something else was going on in my body.

Pain has a purpose. Let's look at how it was used in the Bible. Sarah and Abraham had to experience the pain of Sarah's barrenness in order to better understand the process of waiting and trusting in God for the promise. When they became inpatient, they tried to make the promise come forth, but the promise was in God, not in them. It was only when they learned to wait and trust in God that the thing that they had been waiting on was able to come forth. Then later Abraham had to endure the pain of having to sacrifice his son, Isaac. He was being asked to sacrifice his promise. God intervened on his behalf, but how many of us have been required to sacrifice your promise so that God could get the greater glory? The purpose in that type of sacrifice was to see how much you love and trust God. Do you love him enough to give up the thing that is most precious to you? This is where Abraham was and this is what God is asking us today.

Let's look at Joseph. He was described as the son that Jacob loved most and his other brothers knew this. As a result, they stole his coat of many colors, threw him in a ditch, sold him into slavery and lied to their father, telling him that Joseph was dead. Joseph not only had to endure the pain of hatred and betrayal from his brothers, but he had to deal with being separated from his father whom he loved, being falsely accused, and being placed in jail for a crime that he did not commit. Little did he know that all of this was working for his good. There was a purpose to all of this. When a famine hit the land and Joseph was now serving as governor of the land, his brothers had to come to him for help. They did not know who he was at first, but after he revealed himself to them in Genesis 45:7-8 he says,

"And God sent me before you to preserve you posterity in the earth and to save your lives by a great deliverance. So now it was not you that sent me hither, but God . . ."

There was a purpose to all that he had gone through—it was to save lives. It is the same with us today. The things that we go through, the issues that we face are not just for us, but it is so that we can help somebody else. We endure pain to make us stronger and to better equip us to save someone else's life. David had to endure the pain of rejection from his father and from Saul in order to fulfill his destiny as king. Sometimes when you are chosen, you have to endure affliction, rejection, and your life being at stake just for the sake of Christ.

Look at the woman with the issue of blood. For 12 years she endured the physical pain and fatigue that were symptoms of her ailment. For 12 years she had to endure the mental anguish of being isolated from her friends and family. She had to deal with being ridiculed and being considered an outcast because of her affliction. Even in the midst of all that, there was a purpose in it. She used all her money to seek medical help and was getting worse, yet she never stopped hoping in God. It was her faith in God that caused her to get in a press to go after her healing. She had been dealing with that issue too long and knew that it was time to go after her deliverance. What purpose did her pain serve? Well it allowed us to know that **our faith has the ability to take us from a place of hurting to a place of wholeness**. We have the ability to cause our issues to be subject when we exercise our faith in the power of the Holy Ghost. It teaches us the lesson that **your faith in God must outweigh your pain.** You have got to take on the attitude, I'm hurting, but I trust God. Death is all around me, but I trust God. I have been rejected, scorned, abused, and misunderstood, but I trust God. Your pain can bring you to another level of faith in God.

Psalm 119:71 says, *"It is good for me that I have been afflicted that I might learn thy statutes."* The writer of this Psalm was aware that his afflictions had purpose. Those afflictions pushed him closer to God and caused him to know God at another level. He would have never known God from this dimension had he not had to go through some things and endure some pain. Afflictions help us know and understand that we can't do this on our own. We need God to survive!

In Exodus 1 Joseph is dead and there is a new leader in Egypt who never knew Joseph. He notices that the people of God are great in number, so he comes up with a plan to destroy them before they overtake the Egyptians. The Bible goes on to say that this leader assigns taskmasters to afflict the children of God. This is no different from us. There are some people, some conditions, and some issues that have been assigned to afflict you. These afflictions, adversities, illnesses, problems, conditions did not haphazardly attack you. They have been assigned to you for purpose. You are not just going through—It has been assigned to you for purpose! You are not just hurting or in distress just because—It has been assigned to you for purpose! Yes, some things happened in your life that did not feel good or that caused you to sometimes feel abandoned, unloved, isolated, deserted or forgotten—but it was not by chance. It was assigned to you for purpose!

When you understand the purpose of your pain, you don't have to continue to walk around in sorrow or grief. You don't have to keep holding on to pain. Use it to work purpose in your life. Exodus 1:12 says, *". . . the more they afflicted them, the more they multiplied and grew."* Somebody reading this should be rejoicing because that verse will preach all by itself. Find yourself somebody, call him or her on the phone if you have to and tell him or her, all of this that I am going through is causing me to grow! God is using your pain, your suffering, your frustration, your condition, and your situation to enlarge you in the spirit.

I believe through this God is speaking to someone. You have been dealing with that pain too long. It is time to intensify your faith and move to a place of wholeness. He knows that you were abandoned and because of that you have difficulty trusting people or respecting authority. But it's time to move past that pain so that you can be whole. He knows about the abuse and rejection that you encountered as a child that has contributed to the fact that you have involved yourself in adult relationships that are no good for you. He knows that you had friends who walked away, betrayed you, or talked about you, but it was all to help you grow. It served a purpose. It is making you better. It is time to exercise your faith and release that pain, so that you can be free. Someone else may be dealing with the pain of having to grow up in a home where one sibling was preferred over another, or you are dealing with the resentment of having to take care of your younger sisters and brothers while your parents worked or did whatever and it left you feeling like you were robbed of your childhood. Even worse then that, maybe you had to raise yourself because your parents were never around. Your issue may be different, but the message is still the same. It is time for those issues to be over. You have got to move past your pain into your place deliverance. Your destiny depends on it.

CHAPTER 3

Accepting The Process Of Your Pain

ONE OF THE infallible truths that we must accept is that **pain is a part of our process.** No one is exempt from experiencing some measure of pain during the course of his or her life. The reality is you were conceived through pain and birthed through pain. So why would you think that pain would not be a part of your life? Pain is a part of your process and as my Godfather use to say, "You have got to learn to respect the process." Think about a pregnant woman in labor. The pain of the contractions does two things:

1. It signals that it is time to deliver and that the baby is on the way.
2. It serves as a mechanism or tool used to help push the baby down the birth canal.

This process helps birth new life. If the mother only focused on the pain of the process and not looked toward the end result of the process it might kill her as well as the unborn child. You cannot get stuck in your process, because it will destroy you. Yes, along the way you may have had to struggle and endure some pain, but you have got to accept that pain as a part of your process. You have got to release yourself from becoming so embittered by what you have gone through and understand what it accomplished.

Take the example of Joseph. If he had become bitter and vindictive about what he had to endure, he would have missed his whole purpose for going through. The process that he endured helped to save not only his life, but also the lives of others. I said it before; we go through storms and trials not just for ourselves, but also to help someone else. If Christ had become bitter by being denied by one friend, betrayed by another, and crucified by a group of people (some of which knew he was innocent), he might have stopped the whole process and we would not have the right to eternal life. His ability and determination to endure the process secured life for us. It gave us hope.

Let's look at Rebekah, Isaac's wife. For 20 years she had been barren. When she finally conceived, it was a traumatic event for her. The Bible lets us know in Genesis 25:22 that, *"the children struggled together within her; and she said if it be so, why am I thus?"* In other words what she was asking God was, if this is your will and things are well, then why am I here? Why am I going through like this? Why am I in this place? I am sure that we have all at one time or another wondered the same thing, even if we have never said it out loud. The reality is she was there, in that place of struggle because it was part of her process. She was a vessel used by God to give birth to a promise.

What is the message here? Anybody that is going to be used by God is going to have to endure some pain. The struggle is what qualifies you to be used by God. In answer to Rebekah's question and yours, the reason why you are here is because your purpose is greater than your struggle. You are here because struggles produce promise. You have to endure the struggle and the process of the struggle in order to obtain the promise.

We will never become what God intends for us to become if we don't endure the process. Think about the process of a caterpillar becoming a butterfly. In the in-between stage it goes through a process called metamorphosis. In this process, the caterpillar creates a cocoon. While it is in the cocoon, it goes through a process of change and by the time it comes out of the cocoon shell it has changed in features and in characteristics to a butterfly.

The key factor is if the caterpillar/butterfly does not go through the process properly, it could come out deformed or most importantly it might not survive or make to its intended destiny. What is interesting about this process is that the butterfly has to break through the cocoon. This process of breaking through can be painful. The butterfly struggles to break through the cocoon, but he has to do it in order to become what he is intended to become. The struggle of breaking through is what strengthens him to fly. If he does not go through the process of breaking through, he will die. If someone sees him struggling and tries to break through for him, the butterfly may have the look of a butterfly but it won't have the strength to fly. The struggle is what gives him strength. Pain produces power.

The concept here is no different for us. The struggle of going through is what gives us the strength to go through. It gives us the strength to "fly" and to become what God intended for us to become. If we don't endure, we will have no strength, no power, and we cannot survive without strength. Sure the process seems long and difficult, but go through it so you can live! Pain produces power to live inspite of—! Your survival depends on you making it through the process. You can't get stuck or distracted by your pain because it will cause you to lose focus on why you are going through. Understand that you are here, in this place because of purpose. Purpose is birthed through pain, but it requires a process.

You have got to know that there are some things that could have and should have killed you, but the only reason that they did not was because survival was a part of your process. Not only did God expect you to make it through; he needed you to make it through for the sake of the kingdom. Someone else's survival was depending on your survival. God promised in Isaiah 40 that if you would endure, he would renew your strength and give power to those about to faint. God will not leave us defenseless when we learn to trust him.

Your focus cannot be on the pain of your process, but on what it produced. You cannot focus on the pain of yesterday, but you must use it today to help someone else make it to tomorrow. Yes that drug addiction was intended to kill you, but God kept you alive long enough to deliver you so that you could help someone else get free. Yes, you may have had cancer or some other life threatening illness, but the reason why you are still here is because somebody else needs to know that God is a healer. More importantly someone is still here dealing with their pain but have the testimony like the Hebrew boys that if he doesn't deliver the way we want him to he is still a deliverer and someone else needs to hear that. Some of the things you have encountered made you stronger, so much so that when your next source of opposition came you were able to say, if I could handle that, then surely I can handle this.

Take Jesus on the Cross-. One of the things that he said In Matthew 27:46 was *"Eli, Eli, lama sabachthani-My God, my God why hast thou forsaken me?"* His question was not unlike Rebekah's in Genesis 25. He was ultimately asking if this is your will, then why does it hurt so badly? If this is your will then why does it feel like you have left me? If you are not careful, pain will make you question what you know. God's posture had not changed toward Rebekah or toward Christ nor has it changed toward us. He said in Hebrew 13:5, *"... I will never leave you, nor forsake you."* The process may hurt, but it is necessary. The comfort that we have is that God has promised to be with us.

In Genesis 28:16, Jacob had an encounter with God that led him to the conclusion that, *"Surely the Lord is in this place and I did not know it."* In whatever place you are in, God is with you. He knows the path that you take and in the end you have got to believe that it will all work for your good. Christ's experience on the cross was **on purpose for purpose**. The pain that you have experienced in your life was **on purpose for purpose**.

You have got to know that you are not alone in this. Somebody else is experiencing pain just like you and they need you to come through this so that you can help them through it. Yes that relationship left you devastated and that abuse left you broken. Yes that rejection destroyed your self-esteem and the list of painful events continues, but you have got to forgive your process in order to embrace its purpose. This is why the woman in labor cannot get stuck looking at the pain of the labor because the purpose of the pain is far greater than the pain itself. The process of the pain produces purpose. **If you resent the process, you abort the purpose.** You have to get to the point where when you get through this, you can remember the pain, but like a scar, it does not hurt anymore.

CHAPTER 4

From Hurting To Healing

THE BIBLE TALKS about how Paul and Silas were imprisoned for delivering a woman from the spirit of divination. Divination is derived from the word pythos, which is where the word python originates. A python is a snake that does not kill with a venomous bite, but it squeezes its victim until it literally squeezes the life out of him or her. Many of us are dealing with the same type of spirit in issues, stress, people that are squeezing us to death. The hurt has become so intense that sometimes we don't know which way to go or which way to turn. There are days when you wake up and the pain is so intense that you don't want to get up and it is becoming hard for you to *breathe.*

There are times in the healing process when you are going to have to cry. Crying is not just a way of expressing sorrow, but it is a form of release. Healing requires release and sometimes not just from the pain of it, but from the memory of it. That's why David says, "Create in me a clean heart and renew within me the right spirit." What he shows us is the process of releasing the old and exchanging it for the new.

Sometimes in the process of going from *Hurting To Healing,* you have to let some things go. There are some healings, some deliverances, some breakthroughs, some blessings, some inheritances that we will never be able to fully embrace as long as we hold on to that which has been causing us pain. Sometimes in order to move forward freely, you have got to let some things go. Philippians 3:13 says, *". . . forgetting those things which are behind, and reaching forth unto those thing which are before, I press toward the mark of the high calling of God in Christ Jesus."* There are some things that you have to let go in order to live. Holding on to them could put your destiny in jeopardy. The end result of some of this is death; it has the potential to consume you if you don't let it go. The enemy is trying to abort all that God has spoken concerning you. This is why you must let it go, so that your promises can live. There are people attached to you that need you to live; they are part of your promise and destiny and if you don't let what is hurting you go, what is attached to you will be contaminated and consumed them as well. As long as you hold on to some wounds, you give the enemy strength and power over you. Let it go so you can live. Let it go so you can heal.

Sometimes in the process of healing you must first learn how to worship out of where you are. That is why the psalmist says in Psalm 34, *"I will bless the Lord at all times and his praise shall continually be in my mouth."* An "at all times" praise requires you to praise him in some rough times and some tight places. It says, No matter what my circumstance I am going to bless him because he is still worthy!

You have got to learn to worship out of your pain and anxiety if you want to be healed. You then become like Paul and Silas because your love for God pushes you beyond your pain into his presence. You go beyond the spiritual handcuffs, the open wounds, and the crushing weight of overwhelming situations to seek his face. You may be in a midnight situation, but you can worship because you have hope.

How do you get through your night season? You get through by blessing the name of God. You get through by lifting him up until he becomes greater than any problem. Midnight is a time of transition; it is a time where a change in *season* is about to take place. If you find yourself in a midnight season, don't focus on the pain of it. Just learn to worship because something is about to happen! Worship until the foundations of your prison are shaken. Worship until the chains and shackles around your mind are broken. Worship until you feel release coming your way. When you worship like that, you begin to experience the healing power of God.

You must worship God so intensely that you become desperate for God like Hannah in I Samuel 1. Hannah's circumstance and the intensity of her pain caused her to be so desperate for God that she did whatever she had to get his attention. True worship will get God's attention. The anxiety of her pain drove her into the presence of the Lord. If we are going to go from **a place of hurting to a place of healing** we need the presence of the Lord. Hannah knew that she did not just need something around her she needed something in her. She did not just want a touch she was in need of a change. The only way you can encounter a life changing experience is that you learn how to worship.

Worship allows you to hear directly from God. In II Chronicles 20 King Jehoshaphat knew that if he did not hear from God he would not make it. What was going on around him was bigger than him and it is the same with us. Some of what we deal with on a daily basis is bigger than us—pressure from the job, bills and more bills, a child on drugs, a spouse that has shut down and won't communicate, loss of a loved one, depression, illness, personal addictions and the list goes on; it is too much to handle on your own. Worship allows you to focus on God and not the enemies of your soul. **If we are ever going to be healed, we must learn to spend some uninterrupted time with God.**

Worship has the ability to transform. It can give you victory in a situation that should bring defeat. According to Acts 16, worship transformed a prison cell into a revival. It can cause whatever is holding you captive to loose you and let you go. Worship caused the Hebrew boys to walk out of a fiery furnace unharmed. It can cause something that was intended to destroy you to make you better. In Ezekiel 37, worship caused dry bones to get up and live. Some of your situations have caused you to begin to die mentally, emotionally or spiritually, yet worship has the ability to resurrect you.

In your pursuit of healing you must become like the woman with the alabaster box. That box was symbolic of all she had endured. The content of that box represented sweat, tears, hurt, pain, rejection, abandonment, sickness, sorrow, bad relationships, anger, bitterness, bad decisions, fear, anxiety, guilt, etc. When she entered the room where Jesus was, she knew that she had to break the box because she did not want anything to come between her and her savior. Her attraction to God was greater than the contents of the box. She knew that it was time to be healed. She had been hurting long enough and the only way to get free of the pain was to break its hold over her life. She did that by breaking the box. You do it through worship. Worship is opening the doorway of your soul for an inner healing. It is releasing yourself from anything and anyone that is keeping you from God. If you want to be healed you must go where the master healer is. You only get there through worship.

You must become so desperate for change that you learn how to wrestle with God like Jacob for what you need. You must learn to fight through your experiences and not with your experiences to get what you need from God. Your response must be "I won't let go, I can't let go until you bless me God!"

Stop wrestling with your pain and its causes and learn to wrestle with God! He is the only one that can make your place of struggle your place of victory. **He is the only one that can take you from a place of hurting to a place of healing.**

CHAPTER 5

This Pain May Be Real, But It Is Not Unto Death

IN JOHN 11, the Bible tells the story of Lazarus. He was so sick that his sisters became afraid of what the outcome would be. So, they sent for the one that they knew could bring healing, Jesus. When Jesus heard about Lazarus he said, "This sickness is not unto death, but for the glory of God, that the Son of God might be glorified thereby." The pain you feel may be real, however, as real as it feels your destiny says that it is not unto death. In other words, what you are feeling is not meant to destroy you. Inspite of what you have been feeling mentally, emotionally, or spiritually, death is not the purpose of this pain. The purpose of this pain is that God might be glorified. Where you are may seem overwhelming and there is a part of you that may sometimes wonder what the outcome will be, but know that its purpose is not to destroy you. God is just trying to move miraculously in your life.

John 10:10 says, *". . . I am come that they might have life and that they might have it more abundantly."* Christ purpose for coming was to give life. Without life, you and those connected to you cannot live. It is time that you begin to embrace the life that Christ has given you. Sometimes you have to take another look and see things from God's perspective because the chaos around you and the pain that you feel has the ability to cloud your perception of things. If you take another look, you will see that God is right there with you just like the Hebrew Boys. The thing that could kill you cannot because God is with you. What has the ability to destroy you cannot because God is in control. It is all a part of your destiny.

Job looks for God in the midst of his pain and he comes to the conclusion that even though he was having a hard time seeing God in the midst of his circumstance, he still believed that God knew the way that he took. He was convinced because of his history with God that God was in control and that what was happening in his life was all a part of the plan of God for his life. It did not feel good and it did not make sense, but it was a part of God's plan. Faith operates in the absence of sense. It relies on what you know and is connected to relationship. Job's relationship with God caused him to trust in the fact that God was in control and the same applies to you. Your relationship and your history with God speak to the fact that God is in control of your life. He is the puppet-master. He is the one pulling the strings and if you learn to trust him with your life and your pain, he will ultimately be glorified in your life.

Destiny is a destination that is preordained or predetermined. Its process can be painful, but you cannot allow the pain of your process to confuse what you know about God. According to scripture in Numbers 23:19 it says, *"God is not a man that he should lie."* If he said it then it shall come to pass. Psalm 37:23 says, *"The steps of a good man are ordered by the Lord . . ."* Steps refer to process; ordered steps refer to destiny. There is a process to getting to where you are supposed to be in God. Betrayal was apart of Jesus process. Being rejected was a part of David's process. Being ridiculed was part of Noah's process. Being falsely accused was part of Joseph's process. Being in prison was a part of Paul's process. What pain is part of your process?

Whatever it is, understand that as painful as it may feel, its purpose is not to destroy you. II Corinthians 4:17 says, *"For our light affliction, which is but for a moment worketh for us a far more exceeding and eternal weight of glory . . ."* What that means is that your affliction is working on something greater for you, so let it work. That illness is just so that God can be glorified. That relationship, good or bad, is going to bring God glory. There is glory coming out of this. That hurt is not intended to take you out. It is for the glory of God. That addiction the enemy meant for evil, God is going to somehow turn it around for your good and His glory. Abandoned as a child and rejected as an adult, but God is still going to get the glory. Alone and misunderstood, but God is still going to get the glory.

Often times the process that perfects you is really the thing that hurts or makes no sense to you. Life brings you to places where the pain is so intense that it has no name attached to it. It cannot be classified yet you know it exists. Yet again often times those are the places that cause you to experience the glory of God. Those are the places where you come to know Him on another level. Those are the places where God will reposition you and cause what could have destroyed you to be the thing that causes you to grow.

This pain is not unto death, but that God might get the glory. Just like the Hebrew boys, you furnace has a mouth that is getting ready to testify for you. Your situation and how you go through it is about to speak on your behalf. So, let it testify and allow God to be glorified because the intensity of your circumstance is getting ready to let others know who you and God really are!

CHAPTER 6

This Is Just Temporary

SOMETIMES LIFE IS filled with pain not just around us but also in us. We can't always make sense of it because sometimes it seems like there is no end to it, yet there are two things we have to remember. The first thing to remember is that no matter what we are dealing with, God uses pain to make us who we are and to show us who He is. The second thing to remember is the pain you feel, is just temporary. We serve a God of season and purpose. Suffering has a time frame. As I said before, that is why the scripture says in Ecclesiastes 3:1, *"To everything there is a season, and a time to every purpose under the heaven."* In other words, everything that you encounter in this temporal world has a beginning and an ending. Every purpose has a set time. Every place of pain has a set period of time. Psalm 30:5 says, *". . . Weeping may endure for a night, but joy cometh in the morning."* That just simply means that where I am now is not where I am going to always be. It is turning. This place is temporary. Change is coming.

We have to remember that there is a set time to all of this. What often times becomes so consuming is not just what we are in or what we are dealing with, but the fact that we feel like we have been there too long—hurting too long, stressed too long, broke too long, and the list goes on. When you seem to deal with some things for too long, it can undermine your mentality and warp your perspective. Sometimes other people's dysfunctions can bring disease to your life and malfunction to your existence. When you deal with some things for too long, it has a way of making you dysfunctional which can be painful. We have to be careful that we don't make what God says is temporary, permanent because He has a purpose in mind that we don't want to alter.

In Exodus 14, the children of Israel are in trouble. They are dysfunctional because they have been in bondage too long. When you have been in trouble or pain too long it has the ability to change your vision—you stop seeing yourself the way you should. It has the ability to undermine your self-esteem and blur your vision. You have to be careful because the enemy will try to make your place of suffering permanent when God intended for it to be temporary. Where you are is a place of transition. In the scripture text, Egypt was a place of transition. The children of Israel were stuck; yet the prophecy was their way out; they did not realize it. In the text, God had already said, "400 years you will be in bondage, but after that you are coming out." Just like with them, God has already spoken a word concerning your life and your place in life—this is just temporary. Where you are is just for a season. This temporary place is part of the process. This temporary place has purpose. Where you are is not without purpose; God does not allow anything to occur without a purpose being attached to it. People of purpose have to expect to go through purpose ordained circumstances and situations and it is not always easy. Some things we have endured as part of the purging process because there are some things that we cannot take to the next level. God allows us to go through a process to get out of us the thing that hinders us from going to the next level. This place of assignment you are in not only has purpose attached to it but so does the place itself. Don't be sidetracked by where you are because it is a means of getting you to where you are going. It is just temporary.

There is a turning coming. God is getting ready to intervene and turn it around and make it work for your good. Psalm 30:11 says, *"Thou hast turned for me my mourning into dancing . . ."* Mourning is considered to be grief over loss. Dancing is rejoicing or celebrating. In other words, when this turning comes, that which you have cried over is now going to be the thing that you praise Him the hardest about! That which tried to consume you is going to be the thing that causes you to live! What tried to wipe you out is going to be the thing that now turns around and blesses you! Where you are is just temporary; there is a turning coming! What seemed like it was working against you is getting ready to have to work for you! Your place of struggle, your place of heartache, your place of disappointment, your place of frustration is temporary. There is a turning coming and what you are dealing with is going to come together to work for your good.

As the Word says in 1 Samuel 11:9 (NKJV) when the children of Israel were given a challenge from the enemy, *"Tomorrow, by the time the sun is hot, you shall have help."* That which you are dealing with, that which you are going through is just temporary. Help is on the way! It might be painful but it cannot kill you because you have been promised a tomorrow. What you are facing was just intended for you to see the God of tomorrow. In other words, this pain is temporary in duration, but will have a long-term effect of pushing you to the next level! Hang in there; it is just temporary! There is a tomorrow coming that is going to be better.

CHAPTER 7

Surely, There Is An End To This!

HAVE YOU EVER been in a situation where you kept searching and wondering when it would end? It reminds me of an amusement park. There are some rides that as soon as you get on them you are ready for the ride to be over. I was at an amusement park a few years back and I remember getting on this ride that just spun me around in circles. Very quickly, I developed a discomfort in my stomach and I remember thinking to myself, "*when is this going to end?*"

We encounter things in life where we ask the same question. When will the pain stop? When will I get through this? Will this pain, this suffering ever be over? We get to the place where we become like Jairus in Luke 8:41. His daughter was sick and in trouble and need the master physician so he goes to find Jesus to take him to her, but there is an interruption that seemed to have detained him from getting to the situation. I remember going through a phase where things were happening so fast that I did not have time to take a deep breath. There was one life interruption after another. After going through 18 months of continuous devastation, I remember asking God What was going on? You get to the point where enough is enough! It felt like I was suffocating because the cares of life had become overwhelming. I knew that I was in a place where I needed spiritual and mental resuscitation because life caused me to feel like I was losing consciousness. God spoke clearly and said, "Hold on because there is an end to this, but while you are here don't miss its purpose."

In a moment like that it is easy to ask yourself, how in the world can this have purpose? **The truth of the matter is where you are has a purpose**. What you are going through has a purpose and you must know that it is not to destroy you, but to develop you. God is trying to make you into a vessel that he can use. To do that there must be some breaking, which may include hurt, pain, heartache, tears, suffering, affliction, being misunderstood, being mistreated or being rejected. You must look at all of these things from God's perspective. Instead of walking away wounded, allow the circumstances of life to grow you.

In Luke 22, Jesus sits down with the disciples and tells them of what is to come. He speaks of his upcoming suffering and his impending death. He talks about the fact that one of them will deny him and another will betray him. He concludes this by saying in vs. 37, *". . . this which is written must be accomplished in me . . . for the things concerning me have an end."* In other words, what he was saying was, "where I am has a purpose and an end." He knew that Gethsemane was the beginning of the end of His process and it was painful. Gethsemane is the place of crushing. Gethsemane is the place where you become overwhelmed by the process and the assignment. Suffering is a part of this process; however Jesus knew that if God allowed the suffering, then there was a purpose to it. He understood that he must endure His purpose until the end. The problem with people today is that we do not want to go through anything. The reality is that everything in life has a process that you must go through. You cannot become a doctor or lawyer without going through 8 or more years of education and hands-on-training. We want good jobs, but do not want to do what it takes to get the job.

Christ endured his process because he knew it had an end—desired outcome. Jeremiah 29:11 says, *"For I know the thoughts that I think towards you, saith the Lord, thoughts of peace and not of evil, to give you an expected end."* There is an end to this hurt, this pain, this place of suffering, but you must trust God. Ecclesiastes 7:8 says, *"Better is the end of a thing than the beginning thereof. . ."* Surely there is an end to this because he has promised you something better. Think about what happens when you make a cake. The process requires you to mix butter, eggs, sugar, flour, vanilla, milk, and baking powder together. You put it in a pan and bake it for about an hour and 15 minutes. You let it cool, place it on a cake plate, cut a slice, and then enjoy it! The cut cake represents the end of the process. In the beginning you had the ingredients by themselves in their raw state. Most of the ingredients you would not consume in their raw state. The process that led to the cake as the final product required the ingredients to blend together losing their individual compositions. The blending together as well as enduring the heat of the oven causes ingredients that may be okay individually to be great together, which is the end result of the process. In other words, God requires that we blend with Him. We have to lose our individual composition and mix with Him to become like Him. That process can be painful, yet it is necessary in order for us to become what he has ordained. The end result is better than the beginning, but we must endure the heat—the suffering, the pain—in order to get to the end. If you have encountered anything recently in your life, like me, where you have asked yourself the question, Will this ever be over? the answer from the Lord is **surely, there is an end to this!**

The word surely signifies without a doubt. In the Bible when the word surely is used it is intended to bring a level of confidence to what is being said. Proverbs 23:18 says, *"For surely, there is an end; and thine expectation shall not be cut off."* It does not matter where you are or what you had to go through to get to this place of purpose. Just know that God says surely there is an end to this! You must endure the process, let purpose be fulfilled and watch God do what he said, **For surely, with a certainty, there is an end, an anticipated outcome to this,** but in the meantime do not miss its purpose!

CHAPTER 8

Rename Your Place Of Pain

LIFE HAS A way of finding us in some difficult places. Sometimes we find ourselves so overwhelmed that we cannot catch our breath. Women are carriers by nature; we were created to carry and give birth because within us is a place of nurturing and covering that is innate. Men also have the ability to carry things mentally and emotionally and sometimes it is the weight of what we are carrying that causes our pain.

In Genesis 16, there is a story about two women who were both carrying something. Sarah was carrying the frustration and disappointment of not being able to conceive and give birth, while Hagar was carrying the seed of her master's husband and feelings of brokenness and desolation. Hagar and Sarah were both in pain for different reasons. The pain of these women extended into conflict between them. Sarah could not conceive so she sent her husband unto her servant for her to conceive for her. Hagar became pregnant and Sarah was upset about it so she began to mistreat Hagar. Hagar was a victim of someone else's circumstances and it was overwhelming and very painful. How do you move forward when you feel stuck in the middle? Hagar did not ask to sleep with Abraham nor was she asked. She did not ask to give birth to Abraham's child, yet she finds herself in a place that was very difficult and very painful. You understand this. Some of what you are dealing with you did not ask for. Some of this you do not deserve, yet here you are at one of the most difficult places in your life. What do you do when you get to a place like this? Hagar decides to run. I have an announcement to make—*you cannot run and hide from pain because you carry it with you.* It is in you that is why it has to be handled properly or else it will consume you.

Hagar runs and finds herself in a wilderness. Funny, she was in so much pain that she did not realize that she was running to what was reflectively going on around her and in her—an unsettled place. She tried to take matters in her own hands, but there are some pains that you cannot doctor yourself; you need a specialist to handle your case. Some places we just have to allow God to be God; stand still and watch Him work. We cannot always om our perspective because when you are in pain it is hard to be Hagar finds herself in the wilderness, a place where it is difficult, yet a place where she hears God. Isn't it just like God to speak in at has the ability to kill you, but not the authority? God speaks to her right at her place of pain and instructs her to go back to the place that afflicted her because He has placed something inside of her that will bless her. According to scripture the child she was carrying was Ishmael whose name meant, *"the Lord has heard your affliction."* In other words, her answer was inside of her. Your pain may be real, but your healing is inside of you. *"Greater is He that is in you then he that is in the world."* God speaks to her in the middle of her pain and she is strengthened to continue. God speaks to her in a difficult place where what she feels does not match what she heard yet what she heard changed her perspective about her situation. She finds herself according to verse 13, between Kadesh, which was a wilderness, and Bered, which was like a storm. So Hagar finds herself between a wilderness and a storm then God speaks. She finds herself between an unsettled place and an atmospheric disturbance and God speaks.

Does that sound familiar to any of us? Where you are has you between a wilderness and a storm yet there is purpose there that God is trying to reveal. She became so excited about God speaking to her and giving her what she needs to live that she renames her place of pain, Beerlahairoi, which according to scripture means *"the place I lived through and saw God."* Do not get stuck because of what you feel. Hagar reveals a purpose of pain that we may have never seen before and that is that God expects you to live through this and see Him. In other words, when you come out of this, you will have experienced and been exposed to a different side of God. God wants you to see Him from another level. God sees you and you cannot die here! You have got to see your pain from His perspective and trust in the fact that no matter where you find yourself, he intends for you to leave that place, with life. Position yourself to experience God even in this! It is time rename your place of pain, joy. Rename your place of pain, peace. Rename your place of pain, contentment. Rename your place of pain, strength. Go back rename your place of pain and live!

CHAPTER 9

In The Meantime, Celebrate

IN THE MEANTIME what do you do while you are waiting for purpose to be fulfilled? How do you handle your *now* while you are waiting for your *later* to come? Good questions. You learn to celebrate! Why celebrate? What is there to celebrate? You celebrate the fact that you are still here! Inspite of the pain and suffering, you are still here! Inspite of being misunderstood or rejected, you are still here! You celebrate the fact that what should have killed you did not and what could have stopped you could not because purpose was holding on to you. You celebrate the knowledge that even though people lied on you, talked about you, hurt you or misused you *"No weapon formed against you . . ."* was able to prosper.

What does it mean to celebrate? To celebrate is to honor or praise. So now the question comes, how do you celebrate in the midst of hurting? How do you honor or praise the place that you are in when you still don't understand how you got there? Well you do this by allowing your mind to take a flashback at all that you have encountered in life. You allow yourself to remember the times before when the pain was so great that you should have given up or the times when your head was spinning and your mind was racing so intensely that you should have lost your mind, but God . . . You think on the fact that *"if it had not been for the Lord who was on your side;"* but God . . . You think on the times when you messed up or made a bad decision, but God . . . You think about the times when the doctors had given up and didn't know what to do, but God . . . You think about how you didn't think you would make it after the hurt from the last relationship or how the grief that you endured from the loss of that loved one left such an emptiness that you could not imagine continuing, but God . . . If you live long enough you will experience many close calls and no matter how painful, the fact that you are able to look back at it denotes some sense of victory because whatever it was, it was not able to destroy you. Now that is reason to celebrate!

When I think about this I think about the story of Miriam and the children of Israel in Exodus 14 and 15. These chapters talk about Miriam and the children of Israel as they cross the Red Sea out of Egyptian captivity. The Bible says the sea actually opened up and they were able to cross over on dry land. When they got to the other side they began to sing praises. Miriam took out a tambourine and began to play and sing praises unto God. The other people around her began to follow her lead in praise. They sang, twirled, spun, and danced in honor of what God had done for them. In modern terms, they through a party! They did not know what their next move would be, but they knew they had reason to celebrate. God had prevailed for them once again!

Think about it. When you look back over your life, inspite of where you are now, and think about what God has done for you sometimes you cannot be cute about it. You have just got to do whatever you have got to do:

— Run
— Yell
— Holler
— Jump
— Shout!

Why? Because God has done it again! You celebrate because you realize no matter what has happened, God has been faithful! Your praise of celebration says I trust you God even in this. This celebration is not synchronized or choreographed; it comes out of an experience and a knowing that God is still able! Miriam's praise was prophetic; when you praise God, you act out in the spirit what you expect God to do in the natural. You have to have an expectation that what you have encountered and what has brought you pain is about to manifest something great. Therefore, I celebrate because it is a sign of victory! If it has not manifested yet, it is on the way!

Look at David when he finally brings the Ark of the Covenant back to its rightful place. He becomes so overjoyed as he enters into the city that he dances before the Lord with all his might. There were some people who were close to him that did not understand his praise, but it did not matter to him because he had a reason to celebrate! He was celebrating because he knew something was getting ready to happen. He had not reached his intended destination, but he chose to celebrate because he knew that which he had been waiting on and praying about was on the way! He could celebrate because that which he had suffered for and cried about was about to manifest something greater!

Many of us have been doing this all wrong—we have been waiting for God to do what we need him to do and then we celebrate, but this next miracle, healing, breakthrough, deliverance, promotion, inheritance, assignment, requires you to Celebrate now! As you celebrate, God will begin to release some things! As you celebrate, God will begin to unleash some things! As you celebrate God will begin to restore! As you celebrate, the weight will begin to be lifted! As you celebrate, there is a refreshing that God wants to do in you and through you. Celebrate because you are still here. I don't know when and I don't how, but In The Meantime Celebrate, because your pain is about to manifest something greater!

CHAPTER 10

This Pain Is Birthing Something New

IT IS INTERESTING how we try to maneuver in the midst of discomfort or confusion. Either we struggle with it, try to act like it doesn't exist, or try to deal with it. Trusting God with it is not always a first response, but it will always be the best response. However, that can be difficult when you are in a hard place. Many of you reading this right now have experienced seasons of tremendous warfare; anxiety, confusion, pain, and suffering which can often times challenge our faith. Yet, out of that difficult place God is trying to birth something new. The New Century Version of the Bible in Isaiah 66:8-9 says, *". . . But Jerusalem will give birth to her children just as soon as she feels the birth pains." "In the same way I will not cause pain without allowing something new to be born, says the Lord."*

In other words, I know that you have been in a place of travail and sometimes intense agony, but out of that very hard place, God is about to cause you to give birth to something new—new breakthroughs, new deliverances, new miracles, new gifts, new callings, a new anointing, new ministries, new relationships, new outreach, new businesses, new opportunities, new healings, new assignments, new positions, etc. Do not struggle with the process because it is birthing something greater! The enemy has tried to distract you by what you see and what you feel so much so until it has often times created a disturbance so loud that either you could not hear God or you forgot what he had already spoken, but God clearly wants you to hold on, because this pain, this place of discomfort is about to give birth to something new! There is a purpose here. It may be painful but it is necessary because your pain is getting ready to produce.

In the process though, do not be alarmed if everybody cannot be a witness to this with you because this delivery room only has space for those who are in support of where you are going! That is why God has been pulling on you for time alone with him; He has been pulling on you for a relationship with Him because everybody cannot handle where you are going and what you are about to give birth to.

What you have gone through and endured has prepared you for this! What you have had to face has qualified you for this! The next move of God is getting ready to be birthed through this! Get ready to push! Here it comes—new peace, new joy, new contentment, new deliverance, new healing, new breakthrough, and new fulfillment! Push with your worship; push with your praise—it is time for this to come forth! Push until something happens! Push inspite of your present condition! Push until you know God has heard you! Push until you feel God respond! You must have the kind of encounter where you feel your own water breaking. The Bible says, *"Out of your belly shall flow rivers of living water."* You must push until what comes out of you has the ability to bring healing and deliverance to you and everything connected to you! Push until you feel a release! Push until you give birth to change! Push until God moves for you!

That which you have been feeling has only been labor pain. The frustration, the anxiety, the stress have all been part of the process to get you to this place of delivery. You are in the birthing position and now it is time to give birth to something new. Push past your hurts, your anxieties, your places of rejection, your places of being misunderstood, your frustration, the fatigue, and the stress and begin to worship! It is time to give birth! You have been where you are long enough; it is time to move. What you produce out of this is going to bring a new sense of peace and new sense of order to your life. This pain has a purpose. What you produce out of this is going to give birth to a new level of strength.

Psalm 119:71 the psalmist understood that pain was part of the process to understanding who God is. Your place of pain often times becomes the place where you have to learn to rely solely upon God. It teaches you who you are and who God is to you. It is through these experiences that you not only see him as the God of the circumstance, but also as the God of the solution. When you come out of this you will know God like never before. When you come out of this you will have a greater sense of who you are and what your purpose is. That scripture in Isaiah 66:9 is making reference to the fact that He is not the kind of God to allow you to go through all that you have been through and not produce something out of it. That is the purpose of your pain, to know who God is at deeper level and how He works in your life. It is to understand that the scriptures of old do apply to you now and to know that *"The Lord will perfect that which concerneth* me." It is to help you understand that, "... *he which have begun a good work in you will* perform *it until the day of Jesus Christ.*" Take courage and hang in there. God is trying to show himself in this. He is trying to reveal to you who He is and what He will do. In not many days, something new is coming out of your most difficult place, if it has not already. It has not all been for nothing. Your pain has a purpose attached to it. If you have not seen it yet, hold on because it is coming and when it is complete you will better understand the process and be able to help someone else through it. You will see the purpose of **Pain with a Purpose** fulfilled and you will come to understand that it was painful but necessary. Those places of brokenness and devastation have the potential to become your place of testimony, place of miracle, place of breakthrough, place of restoration. Re-examine your places of pain. Don't linger at the sting of the pain, but persevere through it until you are able to embrace the power of it.

That is what Jesus did on the cross. Every nail was painful and even though the piercing of the spear was after he died, it was still in a sense a mutilation of the body yet it was necessary. God could have shut the hold thing down because after all he is God, yet he knew that there was a greater purpose behind the pain so he suffered it to be so. It was necessary. Christ could not focus on the intensity of the pain, because to do so would have diminished the power behind it. Even at the piercing, the blood and water that came out of him represented life to us. His pain and suffering was producing life for somebody else.

I know that relationship left you hurting. I realize that the abandonment from your parents as a child caused you to grow up as a hurting adult. I realize that the rape and molestation left you hurting emotionally in places that others cannot see or understand. I understand the loss of that loved one has had you in a rough place and some days you were not sure if you were going to make it. I see that you are trying to fight that addiction but the pain of life has tried to keep you in bondage to it. I understand that some of your choices have hurt you or disappointed you and you have been struggling with forgiving yourself. I know that people have lied on you, talked about you, mistreated you, or misunderstood you and the pain of that has left you feeling wounded but in the midst of all of this, there is a purpose. There is a power behind it that is greater than it's sting. Out of this comes strength like you have never known before. Out of this comes more knowledge, more wisdom on how to live life and not just exist. This pain is birthing another level of ministry in you. There are people who are where you have been and they need to see and hear that they can get through this alright. Sometimes we can't minister effectively to it unless we have been through it. This pain is equipping you to do more and go where others won't go to do what others cannot do. There is an assignment connected to this. Trust me, it has not been for nothing. God is using it to develop you; to make you better. Hmmm . . . . I think I can embrace my pain a little better now that I know it is not isolated but it is **Pain With A Purpose**. How about you?

NOTES

* *All Scriptural references are King James Version (KJV) of the Holy Bible unless otherwise noted.*

Preface
1. Matthew 26:38-39

Chapter 1
1. I Kings 3
2. Genesis 4
3. Genesis 6:6-7
4. Genesis 7
5. II Samuel 13-18

Chapter 2
1. Ecclesiastes 3:1
2. Genesis 45:7-8
3. Luke 8:43-48
4. Psalm 119:71
5. Exodus 1

Chapter 3
1. Genesis 25:22
2. Isaiah 40
3. Daniel 3
4. Matthew 27:46
5. Hebrews 13:5
6. Genesis 28:16

Chapter 4
1. Acts 16
2. Philippians 3:13
3. Psalm 34:1
4. I Samuel 1
5. II Chronicles 20
6. Ezekiel 37

Chapter 5
1. John 11
2. John 10:10
3. Numbers 23:19
4. Psalm 37:23
5. II Corinthians 4:17

Chapter 6
1. Ecclesiastes 3:1
2. Psalm 30:5-11
3. Exodus 14
4. I Samuel 11:9 (NKJV)

Chapter 7
1. Luke 8:41
2. Luke 22:34-37
3. Jeremiah 29:11
4. Ecclesiastes 7:8
5. Proverbs 23:18

Chapter 8
1. Genesis 16
2. I John 4:2

Chapter 9
1. Isaiah 54:17
2. Psalm 124:2
3. Exodus 14-15
4. I Samuel 5

Chapter 10
1. Isaiah 66:8-9 (NCV)
2. John 7:38
3. Psalm 119:71
4. Psalm 138:8
5. Philippians 1:6

NKJV= New King James Version NCV= New Century Version

pastorcrs@gmail.com

www.drcrsmith.com

Made in the USA
San Bernardino, CA
08 March 2016